THE SPIRITUAL HEALER'S HANDBOOK

EXPLORING ENERGY MEDICINE

DR. MINAKSHI BANSAL

DEDICATION

To the healers who came before,

whose wisdom and compassion paved the way for
others,

and to the healers yet to come,

who will continue to illuminate the path towards
wholeness.

May this book serve as a guiding light on your
journey.

ррр

Contents

Prayer   *ix*

About The Author   *xi*

Preface   *xv*

1. The Essence Of Energy: Unveiling The Invisible Forces That   1
   Shape Us

Part 1

2. The Healer Within: Awakening Your Innate Ability To Heal   7

Part 2

3. Energy Anatomy 101. Exploring Chakras, Meridians, And   13
   Auras

Part 3

4. Grounding And Centering: The Foundation Of Energy Work   19

Part 4

5. Sensing Subtle Energies: Developing Your Energetic   25
   Sensitivity

Part 5

6. Clearing And Balancing: Techniques For Restoring Energetic   31
   Harmony

Part 6

7. Hands-On Healing: The Power Of Therapeutic Touch   37

Part 7

8. Distance Healing: Sending Energy Across Time And Space   43

Part 8

9. Crystals And Gemstones: Amplifying Healing Energy With   49
   Earth's Treasures

Part 9

Contents

10. Sound Healing: Using Vibration To Harmonize Mind, Body, And Spirit   55

Part 10

11. Nature As Healer: Connecting With The Earth's Energy   61

Part 11

12. Energy And Emotions: The Link Between Feelings And Well-being   67

Part 12

13. Energy And Intuition: Accessing Inner Wisdom For Guidance   73

Part 13

14. Spiritual Protection: Shielding Yourself From Negative Energies   79

Part 14

15. Energy In Relationships: Cultivating Healthy Connections   85

Part 15

16. Energy And The Environment: Our Energetic Impact On The World   91

Part 16

17. Energy And Karma: Understanding The Law Of Cause And Effect   97

Part 17

18. Energy And The Soul: Connecting With Your Higher Self   103

Part 18

19. The Evolution Of Healing: Integrating Energy Medicine Into Modern Life   109

Part 19

Contents

20. The Healer's Journey: A Lifelong Path Of Growth And Service 115

Part 20

21. SUMMARY   121

Citation and References   127

Other Books of the Author   129

CONTACT   135

Prayer

"Om Bhadram Karnebhih Shrinuyama Devah

Bhadram Pashyemakshabhiryajatrah

Sthirairangais Tushtuvamsastanubhih

Vyashema Devahitam Yadayuh

Svasti Na Indro Vriddhashravah

Svasti Nah Pusha Vishwavedah

Svasti Nastarkshyo Arishtanemih

Svasti No Brihaspatir Dadhatu

Om Shantih Shantih Shantih"

This mantra is a prayer for universal well-being, invoking the blessings of various deities for protection, health, and happiness. It emphasizes the importance of experiencing the auspicious through all senses and living a life aligned with divine purpose. The repetition of "Shantih" at the end signifies a deep desire for peace in the individual, the environment, and the universe at large. This mantra is often recited as a prayer for peace, prosperity, and the physical and spiritual well-being of all beings.

᭡᭡᭡

About The Author

This book represents the culmination of extensive research and meticulous analysis, incorporating a diverse range of sources, including numerous books, scholarly studies, and personal experiences. Additionally, I have scoured various websites to gather relevant information and data essential for the compilation of this work. I have taken every precaution to ensure the accuracy of the information presented and have diligently cited all sources to acknowledge their contributions.

From her earliest days, Minakshi was distinguished by an insatiable appetite for reading. Her literary universe was inhabited by characters and narratives that spanned ethical tales, motivational and inspirational stories, and the mythic parables imbued with life lessons. This voracious reading habit was not merely for personal edification but was driven by a desire to distill and disseminate the essence of these narratives to foster the development of students and peers alike. She was particularly captivated by the lives and teachings of historical figures and spiritual leaders such as Adi Shankaracharya, Swami Vivekananda, Dr. APJ Abdul Kalam, Mahamana Pandit Madan Mohan Malviya, Mahatma Gandhi, Sardar Vallabhai Patel, and Vinoba Bhave, among others. Their philosophies and life stories fueled her ambition to embody their ideals of resilience, selflessness, and relentless pursuit of knowledge.

Dr. Minakshi's academic and practical engagement with psychology has been equally noteworthy. As a research scholar, her focus has been on exploring the intricate tapestry of the human psyche, aiming to unlock the potential for psychological well-being and societal harmony. Her scholarly work is complemented by her active involvement in social work, where she employs her academic insights to make tangible differences in the lives of the underprivileged. Her endeavours in social work are characterized by an innovative approach that combines traditional wisdom with contemporary psychological practices to address the multifaceted challenges faced by these communities.

Her artistic talents, another facet of her diverse capabilities, are not merely a personal passion but also serve as a medium through which she communicates and connects with others. Her art, rich in symbolism and emotional depth, reflects her philosophical inquiries and social concerns, offering viewers a glimpse into the breadth of her intellect and the depth of her compassion.

In addition to her contributions to the arts and social sciences, Dr. Minakshi has embraced the healing arts of Pranic Healing, mastering the techniques developed by Master Choa Kok Sui. This practice, which focuses on the manipulation of Prana or life energy to heal the body and aura, has been both a personal journey of discovery and a means through which she extends her healing touch to others. Her proficiency in Pranic Healing is complemented by her advocacy and teaching of various forms of meditation aimed at rejuvenation, personal betterment, and the cultivation of harmony within individuals and communities alike.

Dr. Minakshi's life is a narrative of relentless pursuit, not just of personal achievement but of the upliftment and empowerment of society at large. Her diverse interests and talents—spanning the arts, literature, psychology, and the healing practices—converge on a singular path of service. She embodies the spirit of the luminaries who inspired her, channelling their legacy through her actions and teachings. Through her books, art, and social initiatives, she continues to inspire a new generation to embark on their own journeys of self-discovery, resilience, and altruism.

Her commitment to social betterment, particularly her focus on uplifting underprivileged children, reflects a deep understanding of the transformative potential of education and personal development. By integrating her knowledge of psychology, her artistic sensibilities, and her healing practices, Dr. Bansal has developed a holistic approach to social work that addresses both the immediate needs and the long-term well-being of the communities she serves.

As an author, Dr. Minakshi's writings offer a blend of inspirational insights, practical wisdom, and reflective contemplations drawn from her extensive reading and life experiences. Her books serve as a guide for those seeking to navigate the complexities of life with grace, resilience, and purpose. Through her narratives, she extends an invitation to her readers to explore the depths of their own potential and to contribute meaningfully to the collective well-being of society.

In Dr. Minakshi Bansal, we find a remarkable synthesis of the artist, the scholar, the healer, and the social activist. Her life's work stands as a beacon of hope and a source of inspiration for individuals seeking to make a difference in the world. Her story is a compelling reminder of the power of individual action, rooted in compassion and driven by a profound commitment to the betterment of humanity. Dr. Minakshi's legacy is not just in the tangible outcomes of her efforts but in the enduring spirit of inquiry, empathy, and service that she embodies.

Preface

In the tapestry of human existence, a profound yearning for healing, wholeness, and connection to something greater than ourselves has woven its way through the ages. We seek solace in times of pain, guidance in moments of confusion, and a deeper understanding of the mysteries of life. In this book, I invite you on a journey of exploration and discovery into the realm of energy medicine, an ancient yet ever-evolving field that offers profound insights into the nature of healing and our innate ability to tap into the life force that flows through all of creation.

My own journey into the world of energy medicine began with a personal quest for healing. Years ago, I found myself struggling with chronic pain, fatigue, and a sense of disconnection from my own body and spirit. Conventional medicine offered temporary relief, but it failed to address the root causes of my ailments. In my search for deeper healing, I stumbled upon the world of energy medicine, and it was as if a light had been switched on within me.

Through my studies and personal experiences, I discovered that we are not merely physical beings but energetic beings as well. Our bodies are complex systems of energy, constantly interacting with the environment and with each other. When this energy flow is disrupted or blocked, it can manifest as physical or emotional disease. Energy medicine offers a way to restore balance and harmony to our energy systems, promoting healing on all levels – physical, emotional, mental, and spiritual.

In this book, I have distilled the wisdom and insights I have gained over many years of studying and practicing energy medicine. I have drawn from a wide range of sources, including ancient traditions, modern science, and my own personal experiences, to create a comprehensive guide that will empower you to awaken your own healing potential and connect with the infinite source of healing that resides within you.

This book is not intended to be a substitute for professional medical advice or treatment. Rather, it is a complementary resource that can support your healing journey and empower you to take charge of your own well-being. If you are experiencing any health concerns, it is important to consult with a qualified healthcare practitioner.

In this book, you will explore the fundamental principles of energy medicine, including the nature of energy, the different energy systems of the body, and the various techniques that can be used to clear blockages, balance energy flow, and promote healing. You will learn about the power of intention, the importance of grounding and centering, and the role of intuition in the healing process.

You will also delve into specific energy healing modalities, such as Reiki, Therapeutic Touch, and Healing Touch, and discover how you can use these techniques to heal yourself and others. You will explore the use of crystals and gemstones for healing, learn how to protect yourself from negative energies, and discover the profound connection between energy and our emotions, intuition, and soul.

In this book, you will also discover the healing power of nature and learn how to connect with the earth's energy to promote well-being. You will explore the relationship between energy and karma, understanding the law of cause and effect and how it shapes our experiences and destinies.

Whether you are a seasoned energy healer or new to this field, this book will offer you valuable insights, practical tools, and inspiring stories to support you on your healing journey. It is my hope that this book will empower you to awaken your innate healing potential, deepen your connection to yourself and others, and create a life of greater health, happiness, and fulfillment.

The journey of healing is a lifelong process, a continuous unfolding of our true potential. It is a journey that requires courage, commitment, and a willingness to embrace the unknown. But the rewards are immeasurable. As we awaken to our innate healing abilities, we not only transform our own lives but also contribute to the healing of others and the world around us. We become beacons of light, radiating love, compassion, and healing energy wherever we go.

In this book, I invite you to join me on this journey of discovery, to embrace the power of energy medicine, and to awaken the healer within. May this book be a source of inspiration, guidance, and support as you embark on your own path of healing and transformation.

Dr. Minakshi Bansal
Social Activist
Ahmedabad, Gujarat, Bharat

ᗡᗡᗡ

ONE

THE ESSENCE OF ENERGY: UNVEILING THE INVISIBLE FORCES THAT SHAPE US

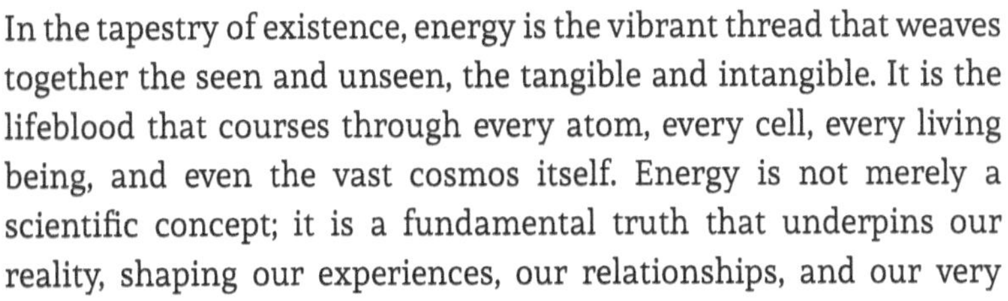

In the tapestry of existence, energy is the vibrant thread that weaves together the seen and unseen, the tangible and intangible. It is the lifeblood that courses through every atom, every cell, every living being, and even the vast cosmos itself. Energy is not merely a scientific concept; it is a fundamental truth that underpins our reality, shaping our experiences, our relationships, and our very being.

At its core, energy is a dynamic force, a vibration, a frequency that resonates throughout the universe. It is not bound by physical form but exists in a multitude of states, from the subtlest whispers to the most powerful roars. This unseen world of energy is a realm of infinite possibilities, where the laws of physics intertwine with the mysteries of consciousness. It is a realm where science and spirituality converge, where ancient wisdom finds validation in modern discoveries.

In the human body, energy flows through intricate pathways, known as meridians, connecting every organ, every tissue, every cell. This vital force, often referred to as "chi" or "prana," animates our physical form, fueling our thoughts, emotions, and actions. It is the spark that ignites our creativity, the fuel that powers our passions, and the source of our vitality. When this energy flows freely and harmoniously, we experience vibrant health, emotional balance, and spiritual well-being. However, when this flow is disrupted or blocked, we may encounter physical ailments, emotional distress, or a sense of spiritual disconnection.

Our energetic field, often referred to as our aura, extends beyond our physical body, radiating outward like a luminous cocoon. This field interacts with the energy of others, the environment, and even the cosmos itself. It is a reflection of our inner state, carrying the imprint of our thoughts, emotions, and experiences. Our aura is not merely a static field; it is a dynamic entity that responds to our environment and our intentions. Through conscious awareness and intentional practice, we can learn to cultivate a vibrant and balanced aura, radiating health, positivity, and well-being.

Beyond our individual energetic fields, there exists a vast interconnected web of energy that permeates all of creation. This cosmic web, sometimes referred to as the "Akashic field" or the "collective unconscious," holds the memory of all that has ever been and all that will ever be. It is a realm of infinite wisdom and potential, where we can tap into the collective consciousness of humanity and the universe itself. By aligning ourselves with this cosmic web, we can access profound insights, guidance, and healing.

The study of energy medicine seeks to understand and harness the power of this unseen world to promote healing and well-being. It recognizes that we are not merely physical beings but energetic beings as well. It acknowledges that our thoughts, emotions, and beliefs have a direct impact on our energetic state and, consequently, our physical health. Through various techniques, such as Reiki, acupuncture, sound healing, and crystal therapy, energy medicine practitioners aim to restore balance and harmony to the body's energy systems, promoting healing on all levels – physical, emotional, mental, and spiritual.

In the realm of energy medicine, the healer acts as a conduit, facilitating the flow of healing energy to the recipient. This energy, whether it originates from the healer's own hands, the earth, the cosmos, or a combination of sources, works to clear blockages, restore balance, and activate the body's innate healing mechanisms. It is a collaborative process, where the healer and recipient work together to create an optimal environment for healing to occur.

Energy medicine is not a replacement for conventional medicine but rather a complementary approach that can work in conjunction with traditional treatments. It offers a holistic perspective on health and well-being, recognizing the interconnectedness of mind, body, and spirit. By addressing the root causes of illness, rather than merely suppressing symptoms, energy medicine can promote lasting healing and transformation.

In the pursuit of optimal health and well-being, it is essential to cultivate an awareness of our energetic nature. By understanding the unseen forces that shape us, we can learn to harness the power of energy to heal ourselves, our relationships, and our world. We can become co-creators of our reality, shaping our experiences through conscious intention and aligned action. As we delve deeper into the mysteries of energy, we embark on a journey of self-discovery, empowerment, and transformation. We awaken to the infinite possibilities that reside within us and the interconnectedness of all life.

᭖᭖᭖

"Energy is the lifeblood of existence, a vibrant dance of unseen forces that shape our reality. Embrace your energetic nature, for within it lies the potential for profound healing and transformation."

TWO

THE HEALER WITHIN: AWAKENING YOUR INNATE ABILITY TO HEAL

Within each of us resides an extraordinary power, a wellspring of healing energy that has the potential to transform our lives and the lives of others. This innate ability to heal is not limited to a select few but is an inherent part of our human nature. It is a gift that we all carry within us, waiting to be awakened and unleashed.

The concept of the "healer within" is rooted in the understanding that we are not merely passive recipients of external healing forces, but active participants in our own well-being. We are not separate from the universal energy that flows through all of creation, but rather, we are an integral part of it. When we recognize and embrace this interconnectedness, we tap into a limitless source of healing potential that resides within us.

This innate ability to heal is not a mystical power reserved for saints and sages, but a natural capacity that can be cultivated and strengthened through conscious awareness and intentional practice. It is a journey of self-discovery, a process of awakening to the wisdom of our bodies, the power of our minds, and the depth of our spirits.

The first step in awakening the healer within is to cultivate a deep sense of self-awareness. This involves paying attention to our thoughts, emotions, and physical sensations, recognizing how they influence our overall well-being. It is about understanding our strengths and weaknesses, our patterns and tendencies, and our unique gifts and challenges. As we become more aware of ourselves, we begin to see the interconnectedness of our mind, body, and spirit, and we gain a deeper understanding of how our thoughts and emotions can either support or hinder our healing process.

Self-care is another essential aspect of awakening the healer within. By nurturing our physical, emotional, and spiritual needs, we create a fertile ground for healing to occur. This may involve practices such as healthy eating, regular exercise, adequate sleep, stress management, and engaging in activities that bring us joy and fulfillment. It is also important to cultivate healthy relationships, surround ourselves with positive influences, and create a supportive environment that fosters our growth and well-being.

As we deepen our self-awareness and practice self-care, we begin to tap into the wisdom of our bodies. Our bodies are incredibly intelligent and possess an innate capacity for self-healing. They communicate with us through sensations, emotions, and intuitive nudges, guiding us towards what we need for optimal health and well-being. By learning to listen to our bodies, we can gain valuable insights into our own healing process and make informed choices that support our well-being.

The power of our minds plays a crucial role in awakening the healer within. Our thoughts and beliefs have a profound impact on our physical and emotional health. By cultivating positive thoughts and beliefs, we create a mental environment that is conducive to healing. This may involve practices such as affirmations, visualization, meditation, and mindfulness. It is also important to challenge negative thoughts and beliefs that may be hindering our healing process and replace them with empowering ones.

The depth of our spirits is another key aspect of awakening the healer within. By connecting with our inner wisdom and intuition, we gain access to a source of guidance and healing that transcends the limitations of the physical world. This may involve practices such as prayer, meditation, contemplation, or spending time in nature. It is about cultivating a sense of awe and wonder for the mysteries of life and recognizing the divine spark that resides within us all.

As we awaken the healer within, we not only heal ourselves but also contribute to the healing of others and the world around us. Our energy, our presence, our words, and our actions can have a profound impact on the people and the environment we interact with. By radiating love, compassion, and healing energy, we become beacons of light, inspiring others to awaken their own healing potential.

The journey of awakening the healer within is a lifelong process, a continuous unfolding of our true potential. It is a journey that requires courage, commitment, and a willingness to embrace the unknown. But the rewards are immeasurable. As we awaken to our innate ability to heal, we not only transform our own lives but also contribute to the healing of the world. We become agents of positive change, co-creating a world that is filled with love, compassion, and well-being.

ᗺᗺᗺ

"The healer within is not a distant dream, but a
dormant power waiting to be awakened. Nurture
your inner wisdom, cultivate compassion, and
unleash your innate ability to heal."

THREE

ENERGY ANATOMY 101. EXPLORING CHAKRAS, MERIDIANS, AND AURAS

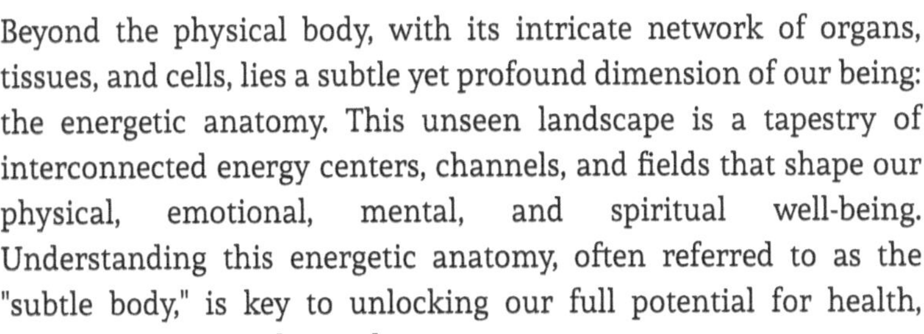

Beyond the physical body, with its intricate network of organs, tissues, and cells, lies a subtle yet profound dimension of our being: the energetic anatomy. This unseen landscape is a tapestry of interconnected energy centers, channels, and fields that shape our physical, emotional, mental, and spiritual well-being. Understanding this energetic anatomy, often referred to as the "subtle body," is key to unlocking our full potential for health, vitality, and spiritual growth.

At the heart of this energetic anatomy are the chakras, whirling vortexes of energy that run along the spine, from the base to the crown of the head. Each chakra is associated with specific physical, emotional, and spiritual aspects of our being. The root chakra, located at the base of the spine, is our foundation, grounding us to the earth and providing a sense of security and stability. The sacral chakra, located in the lower abdomen, governs our creativity, sexuality, and emotional well-being. The solar plexus chakra, situated in the upper abdomen, is our center of personal power, self-esteem, and willpower. The heart chakra, nestled in the center of the chest, is the seat of love, compassion, and forgiveness. The throat chakra, located in the throat, is our center of communication, self-expression, and truth. The third eye chakra, positioned between the eyebrows, is our center of intuition, insight, and spiritual vision. And finally, the crown chakra, located at the top of the head, is our connection to the divine, our sense of oneness with all that is.

When our chakras are open and balanced, energy flows freely through them, nourishing our physical body and supporting our emotional and spiritual well-being. However, when our chakras are blocked or imbalanced, we may experience physical ailments, emotional distress, or a sense of spiritual disconnection. Various practices, such as yoga, meditation, breathwork, and energy healing, can help to clear and balance our chakras, restoring harmony and vitality to our energetic system.

Interwoven with the chakras is a network of energy channels known as meridians. These meridians, like rivers flowing through the landscape of our body, carry the vital life force energy, often referred to as "chi" or "prana," to every cell and organ. This energy is essential for our physical health, emotional balance, and spiritual well-being. When the flow of energy through the meridians is smooth and unobstructed, we experience vibrant health and vitality. However, when the flow is disrupted or blocked, we may encounter physical ailments or emotional distress. Acupuncture, acupressure, and other forms of energy healing can help to clear blockages and restore the smooth flow of energy through the meridians.

Surrounding our physical body is an electromagnetic field known as the aura. This field extends outward from the body, radiating like a luminous cocoon. The aura is not merely a static field; it is a dynamic entity that reflects our inner state, carrying the imprint of our thoughts, emotions, and experiences. The colors, patterns, and vibrations of the aura provide valuable insights into our physical, emotional, and spiritual well-being. By learning to see and interpret the aura, we can gain a deeper understanding of ourselves and others. We can also use this knowledge to identify areas of imbalance or disharmony and take steps to restore balance and promote healing.

The chakras, meridians, and aura are not separate entities but rather interconnected components of a unified energetic system. They work together to maintain our overall health and well-being. When one aspect of this system is out of balance, it can affect the others. For example, a blockage in a chakra may disrupt the flow of energy through the meridians, which in turn may manifest as physical symptoms or emotional distress. Similarly, a weakened aura may leave us vulnerable to negative energies, impacting our physical and emotional health.

By understanding the intricate workings of our energetic anatomy, we can take proactive steps to maintain our health and well-being. We can learn to identify the early signs of imbalance and take corrective action before they manifest as physical or emotional problems. We can also use this knowledge to enhance our spiritual growth and deepen our connection to the divine.

Exploring our energetic anatomy is a journey of self-discovery, a process of awakening to the subtle yet profound dimensions of our being. It is a journey that invites us to look beyond the physical and embrace the unseen, to connect with the wisdom of our bodies, the power of our minds, and the depth of our spirits. It is a journey that leads us to a greater understanding of ourselves, our world, and our place in the cosmos.

❧❧❧

"Chakras, meridians, and auras are not mere concepts, but living maps of our energetic anatomy. Explore these pathways, clear blockages, and restore harmony to your entire being."

FOUR

Grounding and Centering: The Foundation of Energy Work

In the intricate dance of energy healing, grounding and centering serve as the essential foundation upon which all other practices rest. Like the roots of a tree anchoring, it to the earth, grounding connects us to the stabilizing energy of the planet, while centering aligns us with our own inner core, creating a harmonious balance between our inner and outer worlds. These practices are not merely techniques to be performed before and after energy work; they are a way of life, a conscious choice to cultivate stability, clarity, and presence in every moment.

Grounding is the process of connecting our energy to the earth, drawing upon its vast reservoir of strength and stability. It is like plugging into a universal power source, replenishing our energy reserves and releasing any excess or stagnant energy that may be causing imbalance or disharmony. When we are grounded, we feel a sense of rootedness, security, and connection to the physical world.

Our energy is calm, steady, and focused, allowing us to navigate life's challenges with grace and resilience.

There are many ways to practice grounding, each with its own unique benefits. One simple yet effective technique is to walk barefoot on the earth, feeling the cool grass or warm sand beneath our feet. As we walk, we visualize roots extending from the soles of our feet, anchoring us to the earth's core. We imagine drawing up the earth's energy through our roots, filling our bodies with its nourishing and revitalizing force.

Another powerful grounding practice is to sit or lie on the ground, placing our hands palms down on the earth. We close our eyes and visualize energy flowing from the earth, up through our arms, and into our bodies. We feel the earth's energy grounding us, centering us, and filling us with a sense of peace and tranquility.

For those who cannot physically connect with the earth, visualization can be a powerful tool for grounding. We can imagine ourselves standing barefoot on the earth, feeling the texture of the ground beneath our feet, the warmth of the sun on our skin, and the gentle breeze in our hair. We can visualize roots extending from our feet, anchoring us to the earth's core, and energy flowing up from the earth, filling our bodies with its stabilizing and nourishing force.

Centering is the process of aligning ourselves with our own inner core, our center of gravity. It is about finding our balance point, both physically and energetically. When we are centered, we are calm, focused, and present. We are not easily swayed by external circumstances or internal turmoil. We are grounded in our own being, connected to our inner wisdom, and aligned with our purpose.

One way to practice centering is to focus on our breath. As we inhale, we visualize drawing energy up from the earth through our feet and into our bodies. As we exhale, we release any tension or stress, allowing our energy to settle into our center. We continue breathing in this way, focusing on the rise and fall of our abdomen, the sensation of air flowing through our nostrils, and the feeling of grounding and centering that comes with each breath.

Another powerful centering practice is to visualize a white light or a golden ball of energy in the center of our being. We imagine this light radiating outward, filling our entire body with its warm and healing glow. We feel this light grounding us, centering us, and connecting us to our inner wisdom.

Grounding and centering are not one-time practices but ongoing processes that require regular attention and cultivation. The more we practice, the more deeply ingrained these skills become, and the more easily we can access them when we need them most.

By making grounding and centering a regular part of our daily routine, we create a solid foundation for all other energy work. We ensure that our energy is clear, balanced, and aligned, allowing us to channel healing energy more effectively and to receive its benefits more fully. We also create a sense of inner peace, stability, and well-being that radiates outward, positively impacting our relationships, our work, and our overall quality of life.

ᗘᗘᗘ

"Grounding connects us to the earth's stable embrace, anchoring our energy and restoring balance. Centering aligns us with our inner core, guiding us towards clarity and peace."

FIVE

Sensing Subtle Energies: Developing Your Energetic Sensitivity

In the tapestry of existence, there lies a realm beyond the five senses, a subtle yet profound dimension where energy flows, vibrates, and communicates. This is the realm of subtle energies, the unseen forces that shape our reality and connect us to the deeper mysteries of life. Developing our sensitivity to these subtle energies is a journey of self-discovery, a process of awakening to the interconnectedness of all things, and a gateway to profound healing and transformation.

Energetic sensitivity, also known as clairsentience, is the ability to perceive and interpret subtle energies through our physical and intuitive senses. It is a natural capacity that we all possess to varying degrees, but like any skill, it can be honed and developed through practice and awareness. As we cultivate our energetic sensitivity, we become more attuned to the subtle cues and signals that surround us, gaining valuable insights into ourselves, others, and the world around us.

The first step in developing energetic sensitivity is to cultivate a quiet mind and a receptive heart. In the stillness of meditation or mindful awareness, we create a space for subtle energies to reveal themselves. By quieting the chatter of our thoughts and opening our hearts to the present moment, we become more attuned to the subtle vibrations that permeate our being and our environment.

Our physical senses are powerful tools for sensing subtle energies. As we pay attention to our body's sensations, we may notice subtle shifts in temperature, tingling sensations, or a sense of pressure or expansion in certain areas. These physical sensations can provide valuable clues about the energy we are encountering. For example, a feeling of warmth in the heart area may indicate the presence of love and compassion, while a tingling sensation in the hands may signal the flow of healing energy.

Intuition, our inner knowing, is another key aspect of energetic sensitivity. As we learn to trust our gut feelings, hunches, and intuitive nudges, we gain access to a wealth of information that lies beyond the reach of our rational mind. Our intuition can guide us towards people, places, and experiences that support our growth and well-being, and warn us of potential dangers or imbalances.

To further develop our energetic sensitivity, we can engage in practices that enhance our awareness of subtle energies. One such practice is to spend time in nature, attuning ourselves to the rhythms and vibrations of the natural world. As we walk barefoot on the earth, feel the warmth of the sun on our skin, and breathe in the fresh air, we connect with the healing energies of the planet and open ourselves to the subtle messages that nature has to offer.

Another powerful practice is to work with crystals and gemstones, which are known for their ability to amplify and transmit energy. By holding a crystal in our hands or placing it on our body, we can feel its vibrations and tune into its unique energetic properties. Crystals can help to clear blockages, balance our chakras, and enhance our overall energetic sensitivity.

Sound healing is another effective tool for developing energetic sensitivity. The vibrations of sound can penetrate deep into our being, clearing stagnant energy and promoting healing and harmony. By listening to calming music, chanting mantras, or using tuning forks, we can raise our vibration and attune ourselves to the subtle energies of sound.

As we cultivate our energetic sensitivity, it is important to create a safe and supportive environment for our exploration. This may involve setting boundaries with people or situations that drain our energy, practicing self-care, and surrounding ourselves with positive influences. It is also important to trust our intuition and to honor our own unique sensitivities.

Developing energetic sensitivity is an ongoing journey, a process of continuous growth and expansion. As we deepen our awareness and refine our skills, we open ourselves to a world of wonder, healing, and transformation. We discover that we are not separate from the energy that flows through all of creation, but rather, we are an integral part of it. By embracing our energetic sensitivity, we awaken to the interconnectedness of all things and discover our true potential as healers, creators, and co-creators of our reality.

ତତତ

"Intuition is the whisper of your soul, a guiding light that illuminates your path. Learn to listen to its subtle cues and trust its wisdom to navigate life's twists and turns."

SIX

Clearing and Balancing: Techniques for Restoring Energetic Harmony

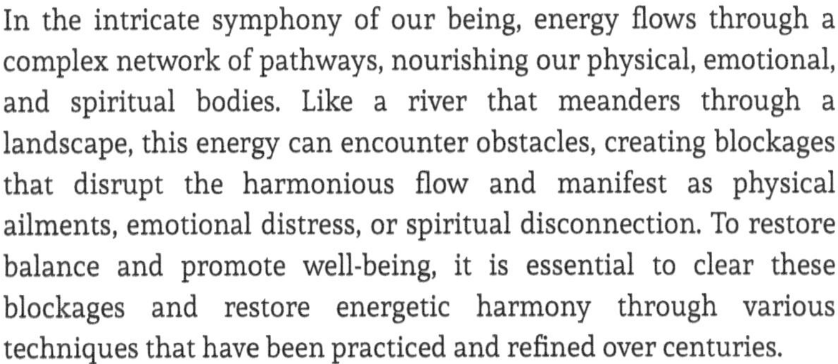

In the intricate symphony of our being, energy flows through a complex network of pathways, nourishing our physical, emotional, and spiritual bodies. Like a river that meanders through a landscape, this energy can encounter obstacles, creating blockages that disrupt the harmonious flow and manifest as physical ailments, emotional distress, or spiritual disconnection. To restore balance and promote well-being, it is essential to clear these blockages and restore energetic harmony through various techniques that have been practiced and refined over centuries.

Clearing and balancing are fundamental practices in energy

medicine, aimed at removing stagnant or negative energy and restoring the natural flow of life force energy within and around us. These techniques work on the premise that our bodies are not merely physical entities but also energetic systems that interact with the environment and other beings. When our energy is clear and balanced, we experience a sense of vitality, well-being, and interconnectedness with the world around us.

One of the most powerful tools for clearing and balancing is breathwork. Our breath is intimately connected to our life force energy, and by consciously regulating our breath, we can influence our energetic state. Deep, rhythmic breathing can help to release tension, calm the mind, and promote the flow of energy throughout the body. Various breathwork techniques, such as pranayama in yoga, alternate nostril breathing, and breath of fire, can be used to clear and balance specific energy centers, or chakras, and to promote overall energetic harmony.

Visualization is another effective technique for clearing and balancing. By creating a mental image of our energy field, we can identify areas of blockage or imbalance and direct our intention towards clearing and restoring them. We can visualize energy flowing freely through our bodies, washing away any negativity or stagnation. We can also visualize ourselves surrounded by a protective shield of light, deflecting any unwanted energies and maintaining our energetic boundaries.

Sound healing is a powerful modality for clearing and balancing. The vibrations of sound can penetrate deep into our being, dislodging stagnant energy and promoting healing and harmony. Singing bowls, tuning forks, and other sound instruments can be used to create specific frequencies that resonate with different energy centers, helping to clear blockages and restore balance. Chanting mantras or simply listening to calming music can also have a profound effect on our energetic state, promoting relaxation, peace, and well-being.

Crystals and gemstones are natural tools for clearing and balancing. Each crystal has its own unique energetic properties that can be harnessed to promote healing and transformation. For example, clear quartz is known for its ability to amplify energy and promote clarity, while amethyst is associated with peace, tranquility, and spiritual connection. By placing crystals on specific energy centers or wearing them as jewelry, we can draw upon their healing vibrations to clear blockages, balance our energy, and enhance our overall well-being.

Energy healing techniques, such as Reiki, Therapeutic Touch, and Healing Touch, involve the practitioner channeling healing energy through their hands to the recipient. This energy works to clear blockages, restore balance, and promote healing on all levels – physical, emotional, mental, and spiritual. Energy healing sessions can be deeply relaxing and rejuvenating, leaving the recipient feeling refreshed, revitalized, and more connected to their inner self.

Nature is a powerful ally in the process of clearing and balancing. Spending time in nature, surrounded by trees, plants, and fresh air, can have a profound effect on our energetic state. The natural world vibrates at a frequency that is harmonious with our own, helping to restore balance and harmony to our energy field. Walking barefoot on the earth, known as "earthing" or "grounding," can also be beneficial, as it allows us to discharge excess energy and draw upon the earth's stabilizing and nourishing energy.

Clearing and balancing are not one-time practices but ongoing processes that require regular attention and care. Just as we brush our teeth and bathe our bodies to maintain physical hygiene, we must also attend to our energetic hygiene to maintain a healthy and balanced state of being. By incorporating these practices into our daily lives, we can cultivate a greater sense of well-being, vitality, and connection to the world around us.

ᗡᗡᗡ

"Clearing and balancing are not one-time events, but ongoing practices that nurture your energetic well-being. Release stagnant energy, embrace fluidity, and create space for healing to unfold."

SEVEN

HANDS-ON HEALING: THE POWER OF THERAPEUTIC TOUCH

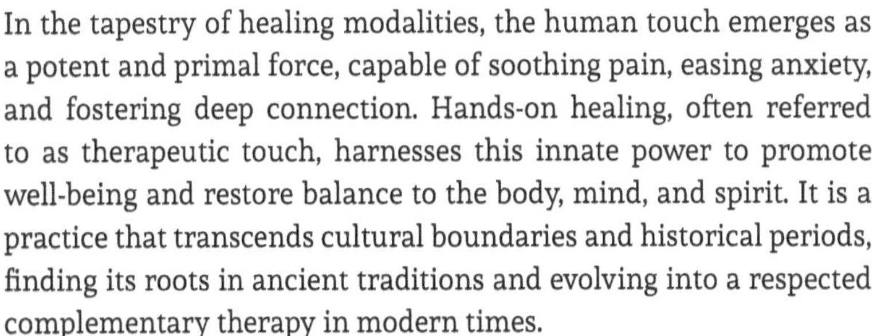

In the tapestry of healing modalities, the human touch emerges as a potent and primal force, capable of soothing pain, easing anxiety, and fostering deep connection. Hands-on healing, often referred to as therapeutic touch, harnesses this innate power to promote well-being and restore balance to the body, mind, and spirit. It is a practice that transcends cultural boundaries and historical periods, finding its roots in ancient traditions and evolving into a respected complementary therapy in modern times.

At its core, hands-on healing is based on the understanding that the human body is not merely a physical entity but also an energy system. This energy, often referred to as "chi" or "prana," flows through a network of channels, or meridians, nourishing every cell and organ. When this flow is disrupted, it can manifest as physical ailments, emotional distress, or spiritual disconnection. Hands-on healing aims to restore the smooth flow of energy, promoting healing and well-being on all levels.

The practice of hands-on healing involves the practitioner placing their hands on or near the recipient's body, often in specific positions corresponding to energy centers, or chakras. The practitioner then channels healing energy through their hands, using various techniques to clear blockages, balance energy flow, and promote relaxation. The recipient may experience a variety of sensations during a session, such as warmth, tingling, or a sense of deep peace and tranquility.

One of the most well-known forms of hands-on healing is Reiki, a Japanese technique that involves the practitioner channeling universal life force energy to the recipient. Reiki practitioners believe that this energy flows through them, guided by their intention to promote healing and well-being. Reiki sessions are typically conducted with the recipient lying down, fully clothed, while the practitioner places their hands on or near the recipient's body in a series of positions.

Therapeutic Touch is another popular form of hands-on healing, developed in the 1970s by Dolores Krieger, a nursing professor. Therapeutic Touch practitioners believe that they can sense the recipient's energy field and use their hands to assess and balance it. They may use various techniques, such as centering, clearing, and modulating the energy field, to promote relaxation, reduce pain, and accelerate healing.

Other forms of hands-on healing include Healing Touch, Polarity Therapy, and Pranic Healing. Each modality has its own unique approach, but they all share the common goal of restoring balance and harmony to the body's energy system through the power of touch.

The benefits of hands-on healing are numerous and varied. On a physical level, it can help to reduce pain, promote relaxation, accelerate healing, and boost the immune system. On an emotional level, it can help to reduce anxiety, stress, and depression, and promote feelings of peace, well-being, and connectedness. On a spiritual level, it can help to deepen self-awareness, connect with inner wisdom, and promote spiritual growth.

Scientific research on hands-on healing is still in its early stages, but preliminary studies have shown promising results. For example, a study published in the Journal of Alternative and Complementary Medicine found that Reiki significantly reduced pain and anxiety in patients undergoing surgery. Another study, published in the journal Pain, found that Therapeutic Touch was effective in reducing pain intensity in patients with chronic pain.

While more research is needed to fully understand the mechanisms by which hands-on healing works, it is clear that it has the potential to be a valuable complementary therapy for a wide range of conditions. If you are considering trying hands-on healing, it is important to choose a qualified practitioner who has been trained in a reputable modality. It is also important to discuss any concerns you may have with your doctor, especially if you are pregnant, have a serious medical condition, or are taking any medications.

Hands-on healing is a gift that we all possess to some degree. By learning to cultivate and channel our healing energy, we can not only promote our own well-being but also contribute to the healing of others and the world around us. Through the power of touch, we can tap into the infinite potential for healing that resides within us all.

ppp

"The power of touch is a sacred gift, a bridge
between hearts and a conduit for healing energy.
Embrace the warmth of therapeutic touch and
witness its transformative effects."

EIGHT

DISTANCE HEALING: SENDING ENERGY ACROSS TIME AND SPACE

Distance healing, an intriguing and powerful modality in the realm of energy medicine, defies the conventional limitations of time and space, allowing healing energy to transcend physical boundaries and reach those in need, regardless of their location. Rooted in the understanding that we are all interconnected through a vast web of energy, distance healing harnesses the power of intention, visualization, and focused awareness to transmit healing vibrations to individuals who may be miles or even continents away.

The concept of distance healing may seem perplexing to some, as it challenges our conventional understanding of how energy works. However, numerous scientific studies have shown that energy can indeed be transmitted across space, even in the absence of physical contact. Quantum physics, for instance, has demonstrated that particles can be entangled, meaning that they are linked in such a way that they can affect each other instantaneously, regardless of the distance between them. Similarly, studies on prayer and distant intention have shown that focused thoughts and intentions can have a measurable impact on living organisms, even from a distance.

Distance healing practitioners believe that we are all connected through a universal field of energy, sometimes referred to as the "quantum field" or the "matrix." This field is not bound by the limitations of time and space, and it is through this field that healing energy can be transmitted. By focusing their intention and visualizing the recipient receiving the healing energy, practitioners can send this energy across space, where it is received and utilized by the recipient's energy field.

There are various techniques for distance healing, each with its own unique approach. Some practitioners use visualization and affirmations, while others use specific hand positions or symbols to channel healing energy. Some modalities, such as Reiki, involve the use of specific symbols and attunements to connect with the universal life force energy, while others, such as Quantum Touch, utilize techniques to amplify the practitioner's own energy field and transmit it to the recipient.

Regardless of the specific technique used, the key to distance healing lies in the practitioner's ability to focus their intention, visualize the recipient receiving the healing energy, and create a clear channel for the energy to flow. This requires a deep level of concentration, compassion, and trust in the healing process. The practitioner must also be able to let go of any attachment to the outcome, allowing the healing energy to do its work without interference.

The recipient of distance healing also plays an important role in the process. By being open and receptive to the healing energy, they create a space for it to be received and utilized by their energy field. This may involve setting aside time for quiet contemplation, meditation, or simply relaxing and allowing the energy to flow.

Distance healing can be used to address a wide range of physical, emotional, and spiritual issues. It can help to reduce pain, promote relaxation, accelerate healing, and boost the immune system. It can also help to reduce anxiety, stress, and depression, and promote feelings of peace, well-being, and connectedness. On a spiritual level, it can help to deepen self-awareness, connect with inner wisdom, and promote spiritual growth.

Distance healing is not a substitute for conventional medical care, but it can be a valuable complementary therapy. It can be used in conjunction with traditional treatments to enhance their effectiveness and promote overall well-being. Distance healing can also be used as a preventative measure, helping to maintain a healthy and balanced state of being.

If you are considering trying distance healing, it is important to choose a qualified practitioner who has been trained in a reputable modality. It is also important to discuss any concerns you may have with your doctor, especially if you are pregnant, have a serious medical condition, or are taking any medications.

Distance healing is a powerful tool for promoting healing and well-being, regardless of physical distance. By harnessing the power of intention, visualization, and focused awareness, we can connect with the universal field of energy and transmit healing vibrations to those in need. Distance healing reminds us that we are all interconnected, and that we have the power to support each other's healing journey, even from afar.

ᛩᛩᛩ

"Distance knows no bounds when it comes to
healing energy. Through intention and compassion,
we can extend our healing touch across time and
space, connecting with those in need."

NINE

CRYSTALS AND GEMSTONES: AMPLIFYING HEALING ENERGY WITH EARTH'S TREASURES

Within the depths of the earth lie treasures of exquisite beauty and profound power – crystals and gemstones. These radiant formations, born from the earth's embrace, hold within them the wisdom of the ages and the vibrational essence of the natural world. For centuries, cultures across the globe have revered crystals and gemstones for their healing properties, utilizing them in rituals, ceremonies, and personal practices to enhance well-being, promote balance, and facilitate spiritual growth.

Crystals and gemstones are more than mere adornments; they are living entities, each with a unique energetic signature and a specific purpose. Formed over millennia through the interplay of heat, pressure, and mineral composition, these geological wonders embody the earth's creative force and the elemental energies that shape our world. Their crystalline structures act as conduits for energy, amplifying, transmitting, and transmuting vibrations to promote healing and transformation.

The use of crystals and gemstones for healing dates back to ancient civilizations, where they were valued for their therapeutic properties and their ability to connect with the spiritual realms. In ancient Egypt, for instance, lapis lazuli was prized for its protective qualities and its ability to enhance intuition and spiritual awareness. In India, Ayurvedic medicine utilizes various gemstones to balance the doshas, or energy types, and promote overall health and well-being.

Modern science is beginning to shed light on the mechanisms by which crystals and gemstones exert their influence. Research has shown that crystals vibrate at specific frequencies, which can interact with the human body's energy field, or aura. These vibrations can help to clear blockages, balance energy flow, and promote healing on a cellular level. Additionally, the chemical composition of crystals can also play a role in their therapeutic properties. For example, amethyst contains trace amounts of iron, which is believed to contribute to its calming and soothing effects.

Each crystal and gemstone possesses unique properties that can be harnessed for specific purposes. Clear quartz, for instance, is known as the "master healer" due to its ability to amplify energy and promote clarity. Amethyst is often used for calming the mind, promoting restful sleep, and enhancing spiritual connection. Rose quartz is associated with love, compassion, and emotional healing, while citrine is known for its ability to attract abundance and prosperity.

Choosing the right crystal or gemstone is a personal and intuitive process. Some people are drawn to certain stones based on their color, shape, or texture, while others choose based on their specific needs or intentions. It is important to trust your intuition and choose the stones that resonate with you on a deeper level.

There are various ways to work with crystals and gemstones for healing. One common practice is to place them on or near specific energy centers, or chakras, to clear blockages and promote balance. For example, placing a rose quartz on the heart chakra can help to open the heart to love and compassion, while placing a citrine on the solar plexus chakra can help to boost confidence and self-esteem.

Another way to work with crystals is to wear them as jewelry or carry them in a pocket or pouch. This allows you to benefit from their vibrations throughout the day, promoting overall well-being and energetic balance. Crystals can also be used in meditation, placed on an altar, or incorporated into rituals and ceremonies to enhance their energetic properties.

It is important to note that crystals and gemstones are not a substitute for conventional medical care, but they can be a valuable complementary therapy. If you are considering using crystals for healing, it is important to consult with a qualified practitioner who can guide you in their safe and effective use.

The world of crystals and gemstones is vast and fascinating, offering endless possibilities for exploration and discovery. By embracing these earth treasures and incorporating them into our lives, we can tap into their healing power and unlock our full potential for health, happiness, and spiritual fulfillment.

ᐅᐅᐅ

"Earth's treasures, crystals, and gemstones, hold within them the wisdom of the ages. Harness their vibrational essence to amplify healing energy and illuminate your path."

TEN

SOUND HEALING: USING VIBRATION TO HARMONIZE MIND, BODY, AND SPIRIT

In the tapestry of healing modalities, sound emerges as a profound and ancient force, capable of harmonizing the mind, body, and spirit. From the rhythmic drumming of indigenous cultures to the ethereal tones of crystal bowls, sound healing harnesses the power of vibration to promote well-being, restore balance, and awaken a deeper connection to ourselves and the world around us.

Sound is not merely a sensory experience; it is a fundamental aspect of creation, a universal language that speaks to the very core of our being. At its essence, sound is vibration, a rhythmic oscillation of energy that travels through the air and other mediums, creating patterns and frequencies that resonate with our physical, emotional, and spiritual bodies. This resonance can have a profound impact on our well-being, influencing our moods, thoughts, and even our cellular structure.

The human body is composed primarily of water, a medium that is highly receptive to sound vibrations. When we are exposed to sound, whether it be music, chanting, or the gentle hum of nature, these vibrations travel through our bodies, interacting with our cells, organs, and energy systems. This interaction can have a variety of effects, ranging from relaxation and stress reduction to pain relief and enhanced immune function.

One of the fundamental principles of sound healing is entrainment, the process by which two oscillating systems synchronize their rhythms. When we are exposed to sound vibrations that are harmonious and coherent, our bodies naturally entrain to these frequencies, aligning our internal rhythms with the external sound source. This entrainment can have a profound impact on our well-being, as it helps to restore balance and harmony to our physical, emotional, and spiritual bodies.

Sound healing utilizes a variety of instruments and techniques to create specific frequencies and vibrations that promote healing and well-being. Some of the most commonly used instruments include singing bowls, tuning forks, gongs, drums, and chimes. These instruments produce rich and complex sounds that can resonate with different parts of our body and energy field, stimulating healing and transformation.

Singing bowls, for instance, are ancient instruments that have been used for centuries in Tibetan and Himalayan cultures for meditation, healing, and spiritual practices. The bowls are typically made of bronze or crystal and produce a deep, resonant sound when struck or rimmed with a mallet. The vibrations produced by singing bowls can penetrate deep into the body, promoting relaxation, releasing tension, and stimulating the flow of energy.

Tuning forks are another powerful tool for sound healing. These simple yet effective instruments produce pure tones that can be used to balance and harmonize specific energy centers, or chakras. By placing a tuning fork on or near a chakra, the practitioner can transmit the vibrational frequency of the fork to the chakra, helping to clear blockages and restore balance.

Gongs, drums, and chimes are other instruments that can be used to create powerful and transformative soundscapes. The deep, resonant tones of a gong can have a profound effect on the nervous system, inducing a state of deep relaxation and meditation. The rhythmic beats of a drum can awaken our primal energy and connect us to the pulse of the earth. The gentle chimes of a wind chime can create a sense of peace and tranquility, inviting us to let go of stress and worry.

In addition to instruments, sound healing also utilizes vocal techniques, such as chanting, toning, and overtone singing. These practices involve the use of our own voices to create specific sounds and vibrations that resonate with our bodies and energy fields. Chanting mantras, for instance, can help to quiet the mind, focus the attention, and connect with higher states of consciousness. Toning, or vocalizing vowel sounds, can help to balance the chakras and promote healing on a cellular level. Overtone singing, a technique that involves producing multiple tones simultaneously, can create a rich and complex sound that can induce deep relaxation and altered states of consciousness.

Sound healing is a versatile and accessible modality that can be used by anyone, regardless of their age, background, or experience. It can be practiced in a variety of settings, from private sessions with a practitioner to group sound baths and workshops. Whether you are seeking relief from physical pain, emotional distress, or simply looking to deepen your connection to yourself and the world around you, sound healing offers a powerful and transformative path towards well-being and wholeness.

ppp

"Sound is not merely a sensory experience, but a powerful tool for harmonizing mind, body, and spirit. Let the vibrations of sound wash over you, releasing tension and restoring balance."

ELEVEN

NATURE AS HEALER: CONNECTING WITH THE EARTH'S ENERGY

In our modern world, dominated by technology and urban landscapes, we often forget our deep connection to the natural world. Yet, nature remains an ever-present source of healing and rejuvenation, a sanctuary where we can recharge our batteries, restore our balance, and reconnect with our inner selves. From the towering trees of a forest to the gentle waves of the ocean, the earth's energy surrounds us, offering solace, wisdom, and a profound sense of belonging.

Nature has an innate ability to heal and restore us on many levels. The sights, sounds, and smells of the natural world can have a calming and restorative effect on our nervous systems, reducing stress and anxiety and promoting relaxation. The fresh air, rich in oxygen and negative ions, can boost our immune system and enhance our overall well-being. The sunlight, a natural source of vitamin D, plays a crucial role in regulating our mood and promoting healthy sleep patterns.

But nature's healing power goes far beyond its physical benefits. It also speaks to our souls, reminding us of our interconnectedness with all living beings and the earth itself. In the presence of nature, we can shed the burdens of our daily lives and tap into a deeper sense of peace and tranquility. We can reconnect with our inner wisdom, our intuition, and our inherent creativity.

One of the most powerful ways to connect with the earth's energy is through the practice of "grounding" or "earthing." This involves spending time in direct contact with the earth, whether it be walking barefoot on the grass, sitting on a rock, or simply placing our hands on the ground. As we connect with the earth's energy, we are able to discharge excess energy and draw upon its stabilizing and nourishing force. This can help to reduce inflammation, improve sleep, and enhance overall well-being.

Another way to connect with nature's healing energy is through the practice of forest bathing, also known as "shinrin-yoku." This Japanese practice involves immersing oneself in the atmosphere of a forest, absorbing the sights, sounds, and smells of the trees and plants. Studies have shown that forest bathing can reduce stress, lower blood pressure, and boost the immune system. It can also enhance creativity, improve mood, and promote a sense of well-being.

Water, another essential element of nature, also holds immense healing power. Whether it be swimming in the ocean, soaking in a hot spring, or simply listening to the sound of a flowing river, water has a way of cleansing and purifying our energy field. It can help to wash away negative emotions, clear mental fog, and promote a sense of renewal and rejuvenation.

The natural world is also home to a vast array of plant and animal life, each with its own unique energetic signature. By spending time in nature and observing the different species that inhabit it, we can learn valuable lessons about life, death, and the interconnectedness of all things. We can also draw upon the healing properties of plants through herbal remedies, aromatherapy, and flower essences.

Connecting with the earth's energy is not only beneficial for our individual well-being but also for the well-being of the planet. As we deepen our relationship with nature, we develop a greater appreciation for its beauty and its importance. We become more mindful of our impact on the environment and more committed to protecting it.

In a world that is increasingly disconnected from nature, it is more important than ever to cultivate our relationship with the earth. By spending time in nature, practicing grounding and earthing, and engaging in activities that connect us to the natural world, we can tap into the healing power of the earth and restore our balance and well-being.

Nature is not merely a backdrop to our lives; it is an integral part of who we are. By embracing our connection to nature, we embrace our own wholeness and tap into the infinite wisdom and healing that it offers.

ᗰᗰᗰ

"Nature is our greatest teacher, a sanctuary for healing and rejuvenation. Immerse yourself in its embrace, breathe in its essence, and reconnect with the wisdom of the earth."

TWELVE

ENERGY AND EMOTIONS: THE LINK BETWEEN FEELINGS AND WELL-BEING

The intricate dance between energy and emotions forms a profound tapestry that shapes our well-being and our experience of the world. Emotions are not merely abstract concepts or fleeting sensations; they are dynamic expressions of energy, vibrating within us and radiating outward into the world. This intricate link between energy and emotions holds the key to understanding our well-being and unlocking our full potential for health, happiness, and fulfillment.

At its core, energy is the life force that animates our being, flowing through our bodies and minds, connecting us to ourselves, others, and the universe. This energy is not static but dynamic, constantly shifting and changing in response to our thoughts, feelings, and experiences. Emotions, in turn, are energetic expressions of these shifts and changes, reflecting the underlying currents of our inner world.

Each emotion carries a unique energetic signature, a specific vibration that resonates within us and influences our overall state of being. Positive emotions, such as joy, love, gratitude, and compassion, vibrate at higher frequencies, generating feelings of lightness, expansion, and well-being. Negative emotions, such as anger, fear, sadness, and resentment, vibrate at lower frequencies, creating feelings of heaviness, contraction, and discomfort.

Our emotional state is not simply a matter of chance; it is a direct reflection of the energy that flows through us. When our energy is clear and balanced, we tend to experience more positive emotions, such as joy, peace, and contentment. However, when our energy is blocked or stagnant, we are more prone to experiencing negative emotions, such as anger, anxiety, and depression.

The link between energy and emotions is a two-way street. Just as our emotions are influenced by our energy, our energy is also influenced by our emotions. When we experience positive emotions, we raise our vibrational frequency, attracting more positive energy into our lives. Conversely, when we experience negative emotions, we lower our vibrational frequency, attracting more negative energy.

This creates a feedback loop, where our emotions and energy continually reinforce each other. If we are caught in a cycle of negative emotions, it can be difficult to break free, as our low vibrational frequency continues to attract more negativity. However, by consciously choosing to focus on positive emotions and cultivate a higher vibrational state, we can shift this dynamic and create a more positive and empowering experience of life.

There are various tools and techniques that we can utilize to manage our emotions and cultivate a more balanced and harmonious energetic state. One of the most powerful tools is mindfulness, the practice of paying non-judgmental attention to our present-moment experience. By cultivating mindfulness, we become more aware of our emotions as they arise, allowing us to observe them without getting caught up in them. This creates a space for us to respond to our emotions in a more skillful and compassionate way, rather than reacting impulsively or suppressing them.

Another powerful tool is energy healing, which involves working with the body's energy system to clear blockages, balance energy flow, and promote healing on all levels. Energy healing modalities, such as Reiki, Therapeutic Touch, and Emotional Freedom Technique (EFT), can be highly effective in releasing trapped emotions, calming the nervous system, and restoring energetic harmony.

Self-care practices, such as healthy eating, regular exercise, adequate sleep, and spending time in nature, are also essential for maintaining a balanced and harmonious energetic state. These practices nourish our bodies and minds, providing the foundation for emotional well-being.

By understanding the link between energy and emotions, we can take charge of our well-being and create a more positive and empowering experience of life. We can learn to recognize the energetic signatures of different emotions, cultivate practices that promote positive emotions and raise our vibrational frequency, and release negative emotions that may be hindering our growth and well-being. By doing so, we not only enhance our own well-being but also contribute to the well-being of those around us, creating a ripple effect of positive energy that extends far beyond ourselves.

ᢒᢒᢒ

"Emotions are not fleeting sensations, but energetic expressions that shape our well-being. Embrace your emotions with compassion, for they hold valuable lessons and guide you towards healing."

THIRTEEN

Energy and Intuition: Accessing Inner Wisdom for Guidance

In the depths of our being, beyond the realm of rational thought and logical analysis, lies a profound wellspring of wisdom and guidance known as intuition. Often described as a "gut feeling" or a "sixth sense," intuition is an inner knowing that transcends the limitations of our conscious mind, offering insights and guidance that can illuminate our path and lead us towards greater fulfillment and well-being. This innate wisdom is intimately connected to our energy, flowing through us like a subtle current, guiding us towards choices and actions that align with our highest good.

Intuition is not a mystical power reserved for a select few, but a natural capacity that we all possess. It is a whisper from our soul, a gentle nudge from the universe, guiding us towards our true path.

Yet, in our modern world, where we are bombarded with information and stimuli, it can be easy to lose touch with this inner wisdom. We may become so caught up in the external world that we forget to listen to the quiet voice within.

The key to accessing our intuition lies in cultivating a deeper connection to our energy. Our energy is not merely a physical force; it is a dynamic and intelligent field that carries information about ourselves, others, and the world around us. By learning to tune into this energetic field, we can access a wealth of wisdom and guidance that can help us navigate life's challenges and make choices that align with our highest good.

One of the most powerful ways to connect with our intuition is through the practice of mindfulness. By paying non-judgmental attention to our present-moment experience, we create a space for our intuition to emerge. As we quiet the chatter of our minds and open ourselves to the present moment, we become more receptive to the subtle whispers of our inner wisdom.

Meditation is another powerful tool for accessing intuition. By stilling the mind and focusing our attention inward, we can tap into the deeper layers of our being, where intuition resides. As we meditate, we may receive insights, images, or feelings that offer guidance or clarity on a particular situation.

Spending time in nature can also enhance our intuition. The natural world vibrates at a frequency that is harmonious with our own, helping to calm our minds and open our hearts. As we connect with the earth's energy, we become more attuned to the subtle cues and signals that nature has to offer.

In addition to these practices, there are also specific techniques that can be used to access intuition. One such technique is muscle testing, also known as applied kinesiology. This involves using the body's subtle muscle responses to answer yes or no questions. By asking a question and observing the body's response, we can tap into our subconscious mind and access our intuitive knowing.

Another technique is pendulum dowsing, which involves using a pendulum to receive answers to questions. The pendulum swings in different directions in response to our questions, providing us with intuitive guidance.

It is important to note that intuition is not always clear-cut or easy to interpret. Sometimes, our intuitive knowing may come in the form of a vague feeling, a fleeting image, or a subtle sensation. It is important to trust these subtle cues and to learn to discern the difference between intuition and fear or wishful thinking.

As we cultivate our intuition, it is also important to remember that it is not a substitute for logic and reason. Intuition is a valuable tool that can complement our rational mind, offering insights and perspectives that we may not have considered otherwise. By integrating our intuition with our logical mind, we can make more informed and empowered choices that align with our highest good.

Intuition is a gift that we all possess, a guiding light that can illuminate our path and lead us towards greater fulfillment and well-being. By cultivating a deeper connection to our energy and learning to trust our inner wisdom, we can tap into this powerful resource and unlock our full potential for living a life of purpose, meaning, and joy.

ｐｐｐ

"Intuition is your compass, your inner GPS that guides you towards your highest good. Trust its whispers, follow its lead, and unlock the wisdom that resides within."

FOURTEEN

SPIRITUAL PROTECTION: SHIELDING YOURSELF FROM NEGATIVE ENERGIES

In the tapestry of spiritual growth and energetic well-being, the concept of spiritual protection emerges as a fundamental practice. It acknowledges that just as we nurture our physical bodies with healthy habits and safeguard them from harm, our energetic and spiritual selves also require protection from negative influences. Spiritual protection is not about fear or isolation, but rather a conscious choice to create a safe and sacred space for ourselves, where we can thrive and flourish.

Energy is ubiquitous, flowing through us, around us, and connecting us to everything and everyone. This energy can be positive, uplifting, and nourishing, or it can be negative, draining, and disruptive. Negative energies can manifest in various forms, such as toxic environments, challenging relationships, or internalized beliefs and emotions. While it is impossible to completely avoid negative energies, we can learn to protect ourselves from their harmful effects and maintain our energetic integrity.

Spiritual protection involves cultivating a strong sense of self-awareness and a deep connection to our inner wisdom. By listening to our intuition, we can discern which energies are beneficial and which are detrimental to our well-being. This discernment allows us to make conscious choices about who and what we allow into our energetic space.

One of the most effective ways to protect ourselves from negative energies is to set clear boundaries. This involves defining what we are willing and unwilling to tolerate in our relationships, our work, and our lives in general. It means learning to say "no" to situations or people that drain our energy or compromise our values. It also means creating physical and energetic boundaries that protect us from unwanted intrusions.

Visualization is a powerful tool for spiritual protection. By imagining ourselves surrounded by a protective shield of light, we create a barrier that deflects negative energies. This shield can be visualized as a white light, a golden bubble, or any other image that resonates with us. As we visualize this shield, we affirm our intention to be protected and to maintain our energetic integrity.

Prayer and meditation are also effective ways to strengthen our spiritual protection. By connecting with our higher power, we can access a source of divine protection and guidance. Through prayer, we can ask for protection and guidance, while meditation can help us to cultivate a state of inner peace and stillness that allows us to remain centered and grounded in the face of negativity.

Crystals and gemstones can also be used for spiritual protection. Certain stones, such as black tourmaline, smoky quartz, and obsidian, are known for their ability to absorb and transmute negative energy. By wearing or carrying these stones, we can create a protective energetic barrier around us.

Smudging is another ancient practice that can be used for spiritual protection. This involves burning sacred herbs, such as sage, cedar, or sweetgrass, and allowing the smoke to cleanse our energy field and our surroundings. Smudging can help to clear negative energy, purify the air, and create a sacred space for healing and transformation.

In addition to these specific techniques, there are also lifestyle practices that can enhance our spiritual protection. These include maintaining a healthy diet, getting adequate sleep, exercising regularly, and spending time in nature. By taking care of our physical bodies, we also strengthen our energetic bodies, making them more resilient to negative influences.

Cultivating positive emotions, such as gratitude, joy, and compassion, is another important aspect of spiritual protection. These emotions raise our vibrational frequency, making it more difficult for lower vibrational energies to affect us. By focusing on the positive, we create an energetic field that is less attractive to negativity.

Spiritual protection is not a one-time event but an ongoing practice. It requires a commitment to self-awareness, self-care, and a willingness to set boundaries and make choices that support our well-being. By incorporating these practices into our daily lives, we can create a sacred space for ourselves, where we can thrive, flourish, and fulfill our highest potential.

ppp

"Spiritual protection is not about fear, but empowerment. Create a sacred space for yourself, set healthy boundaries, and shield your energy from negative influences."

FIFTEEN

Energy in Relationships: Cultivating Healthy Connections

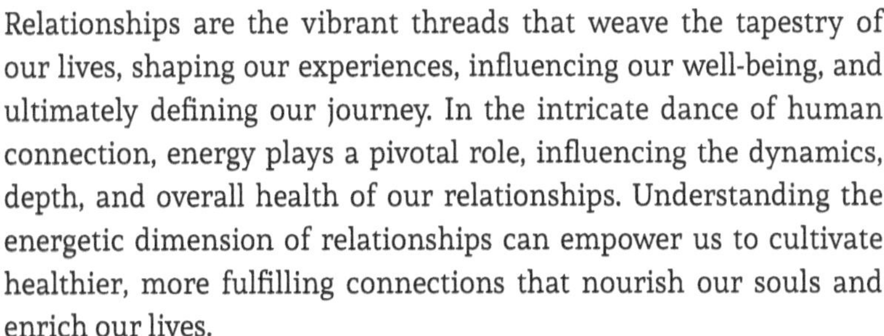

Relationships are the vibrant threads that weave the tapestry of our lives, shaping our experiences, influencing our well-being, and ultimately defining our journey. In the intricate dance of human connection, energy plays a pivotal role, influencing the dynamics, depth, and overall health of our relationships. Understanding the energetic dimension of relationships can empower us to cultivate healthier, more fulfilling connections that nourish our souls and enrich our lives.

At its core, energy is the life force that animates all living beings, flowing through us and connecting us to everything and everyone. In the context of relationships, this energy manifests as an invisible current that flows between individuals, creating a dynamic interplay of emotions, thoughts, and experiences. This energetic exchange can be positive, uplifting, and nourishing, or it can be negative, draining, and depleting.

When we enter into a relationship, our energy fields interact and intertwine, creating a unique energetic dynamic. This dynamic can be harmonious and supportive, fostering a sense of love, trust, and connection. However, it can also be discordant and draining, leading to conflict, misunderstanding, and emotional turmoil.

The quality of our relationships is largely determined by the quality of our energetic exchange. When we approach relationships with an open heart, a clear mind, and a positive intention, we create a space for love, compassion, and understanding to flourish. However, when we approach relationships with fear, judgment, or negativity, we create a space for conflict, resentment, and disconnection.

One of the key factors in cultivating healthy relationships is to become aware of our own energetic state. Our thoughts, emotions, and beliefs all have an energetic signature that we project onto others. If we are filled with negativity, we are likely to attract negative experiences and interactions. Conversely, if we cultivate positive emotions and thoughts, we are more likely to attract positive and uplifting experiences.

Mindfulness is a powerful tool for cultivating awareness of our energetic state. By paying attention to our thoughts, feelings, and bodily sensations in the present moment, we can become more attuned to our own energy and how it affects our relationships. We can also learn to recognize when our energy is being depleted or negatively influenced by others.

Another important aspect of cultivating healthy relationships is to establish clear boundaries. This involves defining what we are willing and unwilling to tolerate in our interactions with others. It means learning to say "no" when necessary and setting limits on how much of our energy we give to others. Boundaries are essential for protecting our own well-being and ensuring that our relationships are based on mutual respect and reciprocity.

Communication is another key factor in cultivating healthy relationships. Open, honest, and compassionate communication allows us to express our needs, share our feelings, and resolve conflicts in a constructive way. It also helps us to build trust and deepen our connection with others.

Forgiveness is an essential ingredient in any healthy relationship. Holding onto resentment and grudges creates a toxic energetic environment that poisons our relationships and harms our own well-being. Forgiveness does not mean condoning hurtful behavior, but rather, it means releasing the negative energy associated with the past and creating space for healing and reconciliation.

Gratitude is another powerful emotion that can enhance our relationships. By expressing gratitude for the people in our lives and the blessings they bring, we cultivate a positive energetic field that attracts more love, joy, and abundance into our relationships.

Cultivating healthy relationships is an ongoing process that requires effort, commitment, and a willingness to learn and grow. By understanding the role of energy in our relationships and utilizing tools such as mindfulness, boundary setting, communication, forgiveness, and gratitude, we can create deeper, more fulfilling connections that nourish our souls and enrich our lives.

ᎠᎠᎠ

"Relationships are energetic exchanges, a dance of connection and growth. Cultivate healthy connections, communicate with compassion, and let love be your guiding light."

SIXTEEN

ENERGY AND THE ENVIRONMENT: OUR ENERGETIC IMPACT ON THE WORLD

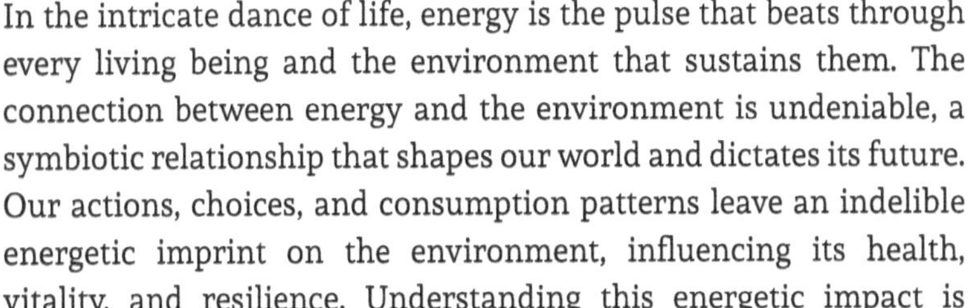

In the intricate dance of life, energy is the pulse that beats through every living being and the environment that sustains them. The connection between energy and the environment is undeniable, a symbiotic relationship that shapes our world and dictates its future. Our actions, choices, and consumption patterns leave an indelible energetic imprint on the environment, influencing its health, vitality, and resilience. Understanding this energetic impact is crucial for fostering a sustainable and harmonious relationship with our planet.

At its core, energy is the life force that powers everything in the universe, from the smallest atom to the vast cosmos. In the context of the environment, energy manifests in various forms, such as solar radiation, wind, water, geothermal heat, and the energy stored in fossil fuels and biomass. These energy sources drive natural processes, sustain ecosystems, and provide the foundation for human civilization.

However, our insatiable demand for energy has led to an unprecedented exploitation of these resources, resulting in profound and often detrimental impacts on the environment. The burning of fossil fuels, for instance, releases greenhouse gases into the atmosphere, contributing to climate change, rising sea levels, and extreme weather events. Deforestation, driven by the demand for land and resources, disrupts ecosystems, reduces biodiversity, and contributes to soil erosion and water pollution.

The extraction and processing of energy resources also have significant environmental impacts. Mining operations can scar the landscape, pollute waterways, and displace communities. The construction of dams and reservoirs can alter river flows, disrupt fish migration patterns, and inundate valuable habitats. The transportation and storage of energy, whether it be oil, gas, or electricity, can also lead to spills, leaks, and other accidents that have devastating consequences for the environment.

But our energetic impact on the environment is not limited to the extraction and consumption of resources. Our thoughts, emotions, and actions also have an energetic effect on the world around us. Negative emotions, such as anger, fear, and resentment, can create a toxic energetic environment that pollutes our surroundings and contributes to disharmony and conflict. Conversely, positive emotions, such as love, compassion, and gratitude, can have a healing and uplifting effect on the environment, promoting peace, harmony, and well-being.

Our collective consciousness also plays a role in shaping the energetic landscape of our planet. When large numbers of people focus their attention and intention on a particular issue, such as peace or environmental protection, they can create a powerful energetic field that can influence events and outcomes. This is the principle behind collective meditation and prayer, which have been shown to have a measurable impact on reducing violence and promoting healing.

To mitigate our energetic impact on the environment, we must adopt a more conscious and responsible approach to energy consumption. This involves reducing our reliance on fossil fuels, transitioning to renewable energy sources, and implementing energy-efficient practices in our homes, businesses, and communities. It also means being mindful of our own energy consumption patterns and making choices that support a sustainable and equitable energy future.

Beyond reducing our energy consumption, we can also actively contribute to the healing of the environment through practices such as energy healing, environmental activism, and conscious consumerism. Energy healing techniques, such as Reiki and Earth healing, can be used to clear negative energies from polluted sites, restore balance to ecosystems, and promote the well-being of the planet. Environmental activism can raise awareness, advocate for policy changes, and inspire collective action to protect the environment. Conscious consumerism involves making choices that support sustainable and ethical businesses and products, reducing our ecological footprint, and voting with our wallets for a healthier planet.

By recognizing our interconnectedness with the environment and taking responsibility for our energetic impact, we can create a more harmonious and sustainable relationship with the earth. We can shift from a mindset of domination and exploitation to one of stewardship and reverence, honoring the earth as a sacred and living entity. We can embrace our role as co-creators of a healthier and more vibrant planet, working together to create a future where both humans and nature can thrive.

ϱϱϱ

"Our actions ripple through the interconnected web of life, leaving an energetic imprint on the environment. Choose wisely, consume consciously, and tread lightly upon the earth."

SEVENTEEN
Energy and Karma: Understanding the Law of Cause and Effect

Energy and karma, two seemingly disparate concepts, are intricately intertwined, forming a fundamental principle that governs the universe and shapes our individual experiences. Karma, often misunderstood as a system of reward and punishment, is essentially the law of cause and effect, the principle that every action, thought, and intention generates a corresponding energetic ripple that ultimately returns to us. This energetic exchange, a continuous dance of cause and effect, weaves the tapestry of our lives, shaping our destinies and guiding our evolution.

At its core, energy is the fundamental building block of the universe, the life force that animates all things. It exists in various forms, from the subtle vibrations of thoughts and emotions to the kinetic energy of physical movement. Every action we take, every word we speak, every thought we think, generates an energetic impulse that reverberates through the cosmos.

Karma is the principle that these energetic impulses do not simply dissipate into the void but rather create a ripple effect that ultimately returns to us. In essence, we are constantly sowing seeds through our actions, thoughts, and intentions, and these seeds will eventually bear fruit, either in this lifetime or in future lifetimes. This is not a matter of fate or predestination, but rather a natural consequence of the interconnectedness of all things.

The law of karma operates on all levels of our being – physical, emotional, mental, and spiritual. On the physical level, our actions can have direct consequences for our bodies and the world around us. For example, if we engage in unhealthy habits, such as smoking or overeating, we may experience physical ailments as a result. On the emotional level, our thoughts and emotions can create energetic patterns that attract similar experiences into our lives. If we harbor anger and resentment, we may find ourselves attracting situations that trigger those emotions. On the mental level, our beliefs and attitudes can shape our perception of reality and influence our choices and actions. If we believe that we are unworthy or incapable, we may create self-fulfilling prophecies that limit our potential. On the spiritual level, our karma is the sum total of our actions, thoughts, and intentions over many lifetimes, shaping our soul's journey and evolution.

Understanding the law of karma can be both empowering and liberating. It reminds us that we are not victims of circumstance but active creators of our own reality. By choosing our actions, thoughts, and intentions wisely, we can create positive karma that will lead to greater happiness, fulfillment, and well-being. It also encourages us to take responsibility for our actions and their consequences, recognizing that we are accountable for the energy we put out into the world.

However, karma is not simply a matter of avoiding negative actions and cultivating positive ones. It is also about learning from our mistakes and using them as opportunities for growth and transformation. When we encounter challenges or setbacks, we can view them as karmic lessons, offering us valuable insights into our own patterns and tendencies. By embracing these challenges with humility and a willingness to learn, we can transform negative karma into positive karma and create a more fulfilling and joyful life.

The law of karma also reminds us that we are not alone in this journey. We are all interconnected, and our actions have a ripple effect that extends far beyond ourselves. By acting with kindness, compassion, and generosity, we create positive karma that benefits not only ourselves but also those around us and the world as a whole.

Ultimately, karma is a force for good, guiding us towards our highest potential and helping us to create a more harmonious and balanced world. By understanding and embracing the law of cause and effect, we can cultivate a life of purpose, meaning, and joy, knowing that we are active participants in the unfolding of our own destiny.

ᐅᐅᐅ

"Karma is not punishment, but a universal law of cause and effect. Every action, thought, and intention sets in motion an energetic ripple that returns to you. Choose wisely."

EIGHTEEN

ENERGY AND THE SOUL: CONNECTING WITH YOUR HIGHER SELF

In the tapestry of human existence, the soul emerges as a luminous thread, weaving together our physical, emotional, and spiritual experiences into a tapestry of profound meaning and purpose. This essence of our being, often referred to as our "higher self," is the seat of our wisdom, intuition, and divine connection. It is the source of our deepest desires, our greatest aspirations, and our most profound insights. Connecting with our higher self is a journey of self-discovery, a process of awakening to our true nature, and a path towards greater fulfillment, peace, and joy.

At its core, energy is the life force that animates all things, flowing through us and connecting us to everything and everyone. This energy is not limited to our physical bodies but extends beyond, encompassing our emotions, thoughts, and spiritual essence. The soul, often described as a spark of divine light, is the highest expression of this energy within us. It is the part of us that transcends the limitations of the physical world, connecting us to a greater reality of infinite possibilities.

The concept of the higher self varies across different spiritual traditions, but it is generally understood as the most authentic and evolved aspect of our being. It is the part of us that is always connected to source energy, the divine intelligence that permeates all of creation. The higher self is often described as our inner guide, our wise counsel, and our ultimate source of inspiration and guidance.

Connecting with our higher self is a process of deepening our self-awareness and expanding our consciousness. It involves recognizing and releasing limiting beliefs and patterns that may be blocking us from accessing our full potential. It also involves cultivating practices that help us to quiet the mind, open the heart, and connect with our inner wisdom.

Meditation is one of the most powerful tools for connecting with our higher self. By stilling the mind and focusing our attention inward, we can create a space for our soul to speak to us. Through meditation, we can access deeper levels of awareness, receive guidance and insights, and connect with the boundless love and wisdom that resides within us.

Prayer is another way to connect with our higher self. Whether we pray to a specific deity, to the universe, or simply to our own inner wisdom, prayer allows us to express our gratitude, seek guidance, and surrender our worries and concerns to a higher power. Through prayer, we can tap into the infinite power of love and compassion that is always available to us.

Spending time in nature can also facilitate our connection with our higher self. Nature is a powerful source of inspiration and healing, offering us a glimpse into the divine order of the universe. By immersing ourselves in the beauty and tranquility of nature, we can quiet our minds, open our hearts, and reconnect with our soul's essence.

Creative expression is another avenue for connecting with our higher self. Whether it be through writing, painting, dancing, or any other form of creative expression, we can tap into our inner wisdom and allow our soul to speak through us. Creative expression is a powerful way to access and express our emotions, release blocked energy, and connect with our deepest desires and aspirations.

Energy healing modalities, such as Reiki, Therapeutic Touch, and Healing Touch, can also facilitate our connection with our higher self. These practices involve the channeling of universal life force energy to promote healing and balance on all levels – physical, emotional, mental, and spiritual. By working with these energies, we can clear blockages, raise our vibrational frequency, and open ourselves to the wisdom and guidance of our higher self.

As we deepen our connection with our higher self, we may experience a greater sense of purpose, meaning, and fulfillment in our lives. We may also find that our intuition becomes stronger, our relationships become more harmonious, and our overall well-being improves. By aligning ourselves with the wisdom and guidance of our higher self, we can live a life that is more authentic, joyful, and aligned with our true purpose.

Connecting with our higher self is a journey of self-discovery, a process of awakening to the infinite potential that resides within us. It is a journey that requires courage, commitment, and a willingness to let go of old patterns and beliefs that no longer serve us. But the rewards are immeasurable. As we connect with our higher self, we tap into a source of wisdom, love, and guidance that can transform our lives and lead us towards greater peace, joy, and fulfillment.

ﮒﮒﮒ

"Your soul, a spark of divine light, is your higher self, your truest essence. Connect with this inner wisdom through meditation, prayer, and creative expression."

NINETEEN

THE EVOLUTION OF HEALING: INTEGRATING ENERGY MEDICINE INTO MODERN LIFE

Healing, an innate human pursuit since time immemorial, has evolved throughout history, adapting to the changing needs and understandings of each era. In the tapestry of modern life, where technological advancements and scientific discoveries often dominate the narrative, a profound shift is occurring: the integration of ancient wisdom and energy medicine into mainstream healthcare. This evolution of healing is not a rejection of modern medicine, but rather a complementary approach that acknowledges the interconnectedness of mind, body, and spirit, and seeks to address the root causes of illness rather than merely suppressing symptoms.

The roots of energy medicine can be traced back to ancient

civilizations, where healers and shamans recognized the existence of a subtle energy that flows through all living beings. This life force energy, known by various names such as "chi" or "prana," was believed to be essential for health and vitality. Ancient healing practices, such as acupuncture, Ayurveda, and traditional Chinese medicine, focused on restoring balance and harmony to this energy flow, promoting healing on all levels.

While these ancient practices have endured for centuries, the advent of modern medicine, with its emphasis on scientific rigor and evidence-based treatments, led to a decline in the popularity of energy medicine in the West. However, in recent decades, there has been a resurgence of interest in these ancient modalities, as people seek holistic approaches to health and well-being that address the root causes of illness rather than merely suppressing symptoms.

This resurgence has been fueled by several factors. Firstly, there is a growing recognition that modern medicine, while effective in treating acute illnesses and injuries, often falls short in addressing chronic conditions and complex health issues. Many people are turning to energy medicine as a complementary therapy to address the underlying causes of their ailments, such as stress, emotional trauma, and environmental toxins.

Secondly, there is a growing body of scientific evidence supporting the effectiveness of energy medicine. Studies have shown that practices such as Reiki, acupuncture, and therapeutic touch can reduce pain, anxiety, and stress, boost the immune system, and promote healing on a cellular level. This research has helped to legitimize energy medicine in the eyes of both the public and the medical community, paving the way for its integration into mainstream healthcare.

Thirdly, there is a growing awareness of the interconnectedness of mind, body, and spirit. Modern medicine tends to focus on the physical body, often neglecting the emotional and spiritual dimensions of health. Energy medicine, on the other hand, recognizes the interconnectedness of all aspects of our being and seeks to address the root causes of illness at all levels.

The integration of energy medicine into modern life is not without its challenges. One of the main obstacles is the lack of standardized training and certification for energy medicine practitioners. Unlike conventional medical practitioners, who undergo rigorous training and licensing procedures, energy medicine practitioners often come from diverse backgrounds and may have varying levels of expertise. This can make it difficult for patients to choose a qualified practitioner and can also lead to skepticism and distrust from the medical community.

Another challenge is the lack of insurance coverage for energy medicine treatments. Many insurance companies do not recognize energy medicine as a legitimate form of healthcare, making it inaccessible to many people who cannot afford to pay out of pocket.

Despite these challenges, the integration of energy medicine into modern life is gaining momentum. Many hospitals and clinics are now offering complementary therapies, such as Reiki, acupuncture, and massage, alongside conventional treatments. Some medical schools are even incorporating energy medicine into their curriculum, recognizing its potential to enhance patient care and improve outcomes.

The evolution of healing is a continuous process, a journey of discovery and integration. By embracing the wisdom of ancient traditions and integrating them with the latest scientific advancements, we can create a new paradigm of healthcare that addresses the whole person – body, mind, and spirit. This holistic approach to healing has the potential to transform our lives, our communities, and our world, creating a healthier, happier, and more harmonious future for all.

❧❧❧

"The evolution of healing is a dance between ancient wisdom and modern science. Embrace both, integrate their teachings, and pave the way for a holistic approach to well-being."

TWENTY

THE HEALER'S JOURNEY: A LIFELONG PATH OF GROWTH AND SERVICE

The path of the healer is not merely a profession or a skill set, but a lifelong journey of growth, transformation, and service to others. It is a calling that beckons individuals to step into their fullest potential, to awaken their innate healing abilities, and to share their gifts with the world. The healer's journey is a winding path filled with challenges, triumphs, and profound self-discovery, leading to a life of meaning, purpose, and deep connection to the human spirit.

The journey begins with a spark, an inner knowing that calls us to explore the mysteries of healing and to dedicate our lives to the service of others. This initial spark may be ignited by a personal experience of healing, a desire to help others, or a deep yearning to connect with something greater than ourselves. Regardless of its origin, this spark ignites a fire within us, propelling us forward on a path of exploration and discovery.

The early stages of the healer's journey are often marked by a thirst for knowledge and a deep dive into various healing modalities. We may explore ancient traditions such as Ayurveda, Traditional Chinese Medicine, or Shamanism, or delve into modern practices like Reiki, Therapeutic Touch, or energy psychology. We may attend workshops, read books, or seek out mentors who can guide us on our path. This period of learning and exploration is essential for developing a strong foundation in the principles and practices of healing.

As we deepen our knowledge and understanding, we begin to experiment with different modalities, discovering which ones resonate with us most deeply. We may find that we are drawn to hands-on healing techniques, such as massage or Reiki, or that we prefer to work with energy at a distance through prayer or intention. We may also discover that we have a particular affinity for certain types of clients or conditions. This process of experimentation and self-discovery helps us to refine our skills and develop our unique style as healers.

As we gain experience and confidence, we begin to offer our services to others, sharing our gifts with those who are seeking healing and transformation. This can be a humbling and rewarding experience, as we witness the power of healing energy to transform lives. We may work with clients one-on-one, in group settings, or even at a distance. We may also choose to specialize in a particular area, such as physical healing, emotional healing, or spiritual guidance.

The healer's journey is not without its challenges. We may encounter skepticism, doubt, or resistance from others, including friends, family, and even the medical community. We may also face our own inner demons, such as fear, self-doubt, and imposter syndrome. These challenges can be difficult to navigate, but they also offer opportunities for growth and learning. By facing our fears and doubts head-on, we can strengthen our resolve, deepen our trust in our abilities, and emerge as more resilient and compassionate healers.

As we continue on our journey, we may find ourselves drawn to explore deeper levels of healing, such as ancestral healing, past life regression, or shamanic journeying. We may also develop a deeper understanding of the interconnectedness of all things, recognizing that our own healing is inextricably linked to the healing of the planet and all its inhabitants.

The healer's journey is not a linear path but a spiral, a continuous cycle of learning, growth, and service. As we evolve as healers, we also evolve as human beings, shedding old patterns and beliefs that no longer serve us and embracing new ways of being that align with our highest purpose.

Ultimately, the healer's journey is a path of love, compassion, and service to others. It is a calling that invites us to step into our fullest potential, to embrace our unique gifts, and to share them with the world. As we walk this path, we discover that the true healer resides within us all, waiting to be awakened and unleashed.

ᕱᕱᕱ

"The healer's journey is a lifelong pilgrimage, a continuous unfolding of your true potential. Embrace the challenges, celebrate the triumphs, and serve with an open heart."

TWENTY-ONE
SUMMARY

Energy, the life force that animates all creation, is a profound and multifaceted concept that extends far beyond the realm of physics. It is the vibrant thread that weaves together our physical, emotional, mental, and spiritual experiences, shaping our reality and influencing our well-being.

At the heart of our energetic being lies a complex and interconnected system of energy centers, channels, and fields. The chakras, spinning vortices of energy aligned along the spine, govern different aspects of our physical, emotional, and spiritual health. The meridians, like rivers flowing through our bodies, carry vital life force energy to every cell and organ. The aura, an electromagnetic field that surrounds our bodies, reflects our inner state and interacts with the energy of others and the environment. Understanding this energetic anatomy is crucial for maintaining balance and promoting healing on all levels.

Grounding and centering are fundamental practices in energy work, providing a stable foundation for accessing and working with subtle energies. Grounding connects us to the earth's stabilizing energy, while centering aligns us with our inner core, creating a harmonious balance between our inner and outer worlds. These practices are essential for maintaining clarity, focus, and presence in our daily lives and during energy healing sessions.

Energetic sensitivity, or clairsentience, is the ability to perceive and interpret subtle energies through our physical and intuitive senses. This natural capacity can be cultivated through mindfulness, meditation, spending time in nature, and working with crystals and sound healing. By developing our energetic sensitivity, we can gain valuable insights into ourselves, others, and the world around us, and tap into our innate healing abilities.

Clearing and balancing are essential practices for maintaining energetic harmony. Techniques such as breathwork, visualization, sound healing, crystal therapy, and energy healing can help to remove blockages, restore balance, and promote the smooth flow of energy throughout our bodies. By regularly clearing and balancing our energy, we can prevent dis-ease, enhance our well-being, and deepen our connection to ourselves and the world around us.

Hands-on healing, a powerful modality that utilizes the healing power of touch, has been practiced for centuries across various cultures. This practice involves the practitioner channeling healing energy through their hands to the recipient, promoting relaxation, pain relief, and healing on all levels. Reiki, Therapeutic Touch, and other hands-on healing modalities offer a gentle yet effective way to restore balance and harmony to the body's energy system.

Distance healing, a fascinating and often misunderstood aspect of energy medicine, allows healing energy to transcend physical boundaries and reach those in need, regardless of their location. By focusing their intention and visualizing the recipient receiving healing energy, practitioners can transmit this energy across space, where it is received and utilized by the recipient's energy field. Distance healing can be used to address a wide range of physical, emotional, and spiritual issues, and it is a powerful reminder of our interconnectedness with all beings.

Crystals and gemstones, earth's radiant treasures, hold within them a unique vibrational essence that can be harnessed for healing and transformation. Each crystal possesses specific properties that can be used to clear blockages, balance energy centers, and promote healing on various levels. By working with crystals and gemstones, we can tap into the earth's energy and enhance our own well-being.

Sound healing, an ancient and powerful modality, utilizes the vibrations of sound to harmonize the mind, body, and spirit. Singing bowls, tuning forks, gongs, and other instruments produce specific frequencies that resonate with different parts of our body and energy field, promoting relaxation, releasing tension, and stimulating healing. Sound healing can be used to address a wide range of issues, from physical pain to emotional trauma, and it offers a unique and accessible pathway to well-being.

Nature, the source of all life, offers a profound healing balm for our modern ailments. By spending time in nature, practicing grounding, and connecting with the earth's energy, we can reduce stress, boost our immune system, and enhance our overall well-being. Nature also reminds us of our interconnectedness with all living beings and can inspire a sense of awe, wonder, and gratitude for the beauty and abundance of the natural world.

The intricate link between energy and emotions plays a crucial role in our overall well-being. Our emotions are not merely abstract concepts but are dynamic expressions of energy that vibrate within us and radiate outward. By understanding this link, we can learn to manage our emotions more effectively, cultivate positive emotions, and release negative energy that may be hindering our growth and well-being.

Intuition, our inner knowing, is a powerful guide that can help us navigate life's challenges and make choices that align with our highest good. This innate wisdom is intimately connected to our energy, flowing through us like a subtle current, guiding us towards our true path. By cultivating mindfulness, meditation, and spending time in nature, we can deepen our connection to our intuition and access the profound wisdom that resides within us.

In the intricate dance of cause and effect, energy and karma play a significant role in shaping our experiences and destinies. Karma is the law of cause and effect, the principle that every action, thought, and intention generates a corresponding energetic ripple that ultimately returns to us. By understanding and embracing the law of karma, we can take responsibility for our actions, learn from our mistakes, and create a more positive and fulfilling life.

The soul, the essence of our being, is the highest expression of energy within us. Connecting with our higher self is a journey of self-discovery, a process of awakening to our true nature, and a path towards greater fulfillment, peace, and joy. By cultivating practices such as meditation, prayer, creative expression, and energy healing, we can deepen our connection to our higher self and tap into the infinite wisdom and guidance that resides within us.

As we navigate the complexities of modern life, integrating energy medicine into our healthcare practices offers a holistic approach that addresses the whole person - body, mind, and spirit. This evolution of healing acknowledges the interconnectedness of all aspects of our being and seeks to address the root causes of illness rather than merely suppressing symptoms. By embracing the wisdom of ancient traditions and integrating them with the latest scientific advancements, we can create a new paradigm of healthcare that promotes optimal health, well-being, and spiritual growth.

The healer's journey is a lifelong path of growth, transformation, and service to others. It begins with a spark, an inner knowing that calls us to explore the mysteries of healing and to dedicate our lives to the service of others. As we journey along this path, we encounter challenges, triumphs, and profound self-discovery. By embracing our unique gifts and sharing them with the world, we can make a positive impact on the lives of others and contribute to the healing of the planet.

ᗏᗏᗏ

Citation And References

This book represents the culmination of extensive research and meticulous analysis, incorporating a diverse range of sources, including numerous books, scholarly studies, and personal experiences. Additionally, I have scoured various websites to gather relevant information and data essential for the compilation of this work. I have taken every precaution to ensure the accuracy of the information presented and have diligently cited all sources to acknowledge their contributions.

Despite these efforts, the possibility of inadvertent errors remains. I deeply value the insights of my readers and appreciate any feedback that can help identify and rectify such inaccuracies. I encourage you to bring any discrepancies to my attention.

Your feedback is not only welcome but crucial, as it will aid in correcting current editions and enhancing the content of future ones. I am committed to maintaining the highest standards of accuracy and reliability in my work and thank you for your support and understanding.

Additionally, I firmly uphold the principle of freedom of speech and expression as guaranteed under Article 19(1)(a) of the Constitution of India, and I respect the diverse viewpoints and expressions of all readers.

ϷϷϷ

Other Books Of The Author

1. Empowering Minds: A Journey into Women's Self-Discovery and Power
2. The Dynamics of Motivation: Catalyzing Thought into Action
3. Meditation and Mental Well Being: The Path to Inner Peace and Clarity
4. The Psychology of Child Education: Nurturing Future Generations
5. Ethical Enlightenment: A Modern Guide to Living with Integrity
6. Voices of Empowerment: Stories of Women Rising Against Odds
7. Social Psychology in Everyday Life: Understanding Human Connections
8. The Essence of Motivational Speaking: Inspiring Change in Others
9. Balancing Acts: Women, Work, and the Will to Lead
10. Guiding with Grace: Raising Children with Compassion and Awareness
11. The Power of Positive Aging: Embracing Life After Fifty
12. Building Resilient Communities: Social Work in Action
13. The Ethical Educator: Principles for Teaching and Learning
14. From Insight to Impact: Social Psychology for a Better World
15. The Ethics of Empathy: A Guide to Ethical Living
16. The Science of Empowering the Self: Navigating Life's Challenges with Psychological Wisdom
17. The Mindful Conscious Leader: Meditation Techniques for Modern Management
18. Pioneering Spirit: Women's Pathways to Leadership and Empowerment
19. Feeling to Healing: The Role of Emotional Intelligence in Child Development
20. Transformative Talks and Words of Inspiration: Insights into Motivational Oratory

21. Green Ethics: A Path to Sustainable Living
22. Spiritual Integrity: Navigating Life with Moral Compassion
23. Clean Living, Clean Society: The Ethics of Cleanliness
24. Patriotic Spirits: Building a Nation on Positive Attitudes
25. Innovative Integrity & Vibrant Visions: The Ethical and Entrepreneurial Spirit of Gujarat
26. Youthful Visions, Endless Possibilities: Inspiring Ethics and Motivation in Children
27. Living Your Legacy: How to Motivate Others by Living Your Values
28. Secret of Healing Conversations: Ethical Practices in Counselling and Therapy
29. Creative Kindness: Crafting a Life of Compassion and Creativity
30. The Power of Appreciation: How Gratitude Can Transform Your Relationships
31. Bhagavad-Gita: Messages
32. Science of Art: The New Frontier of Fashion Modernism
33. Vivekananda's Virtues: A Blueprint for Modern Living
34. Empower Her: Navigating the Path to Women's Entrepreneurship
35. The Boundless Classroom: Innovations in Global Education
36. The Language of Leadership: Communicating with Authenticity and Impact
37. The Warrior's Mantra: Deciphering the Hanuman Chalisa
38. Echoes of Empathy: Transformative Stories of Social Service
39. Artful Living: Cultivating Creativity in Your Daily Routine
40. Finding Your Why: Discovering Your Passions and Charting Your Course
41. The Role of Social Media in Shaping Self-Esteem and Interpersonal Relationships among Adolescents
42. Karma's Tapestry: Weaving a Life of Selfless Service
43. Altruistic Alchemy: Transforming Lives Through Giving
44. The Blueprint of Pro-Activeness and Productivity: Crafting Habits for Success
45. The Simplicity with Grounded Wisdom: Embracing Authenticity

in a Complex World

46. Secret of Solopreneur's Odyssey: Navigating the Path to Self-Employment

47. Exploring Tapestry of Peace: Global Perspectives on Harmony

48. The Art and Actions of Connection: Mastering Communication for Impact

49. She Governs and at the Helm: Strategies for Political Empowerment

50. Rising Above and Rising with Grace: A Woman's Roadmap to Career Mastery

51. The Effect of Networking & Connectedness: Building Strategic Alliances for Women

52. Beyond his Barriers: Women Thriving in Male-Dominated Fields

53. Secret of Inner Compass: Navigating Life with Intuition

54. Creative & Pro-Active Muses: A Celebration of Women in the Arts

55. Unburdened: The Art of Releasing the Past

56. Amplified Voices: Speeches of Women that Astonished the World

57. Secret of Manifesting Dreams: A Woman's Guide to Intentional Living

58. Ethics and Value Based Education: Reimagining Japan's School System

59. The Moral Compass Curriculum: A Holistic Approach

60. Tech with Heart: Integrating Ethics into Digital Learning

61. Honoring Virtue: Recognizing Ethical Excellence in Education

62. Raising Good Humans: A Guide to Character Development

63. The Spark Within: Nurturing Creativity in Children

64. The Teenager Whisperer: Navigating Adolescence with Grace

65. Igniting a Passion for Learning: Inspiring Lifelong Curiosity

66. The Habit Lab: Cultivating Positive Behaviors in Children

67. Seeds of Empathy: Fostering Compassion in Young Hearts

68. The Reading Revolution: Inspiring a Love of Books in Children

69. The Learning Brain: Unlocking the Secrets of Student Success

70. Teaching for All: Differentiated Instruction Strategies

71. The Time Alchemist: Mastering Time Management for Peak Performance

72. The Resilience Factor: Transforming Setbacks into Stepping Stones
73. The Healing Touch of Nature: An Introduction to Naturopathy
74. Echoes of the Past: Healing Through Past Life Regression
75. The Spiritual Healer's Handbook: Exploring Energy Medicine
76. Crystal Clarity: Unveiling the Power of Gemstones
77. The Dream Weaver's Guide: Decoding the Language of Dreams
78. Emotional Alchemy: Transforming Pain into Power
79. Sonic Serenity: Harnessing Sound for Stress Relief
80. The Entrepreneur's Playbook: Launching Your Business with Confidence
81. Productivity Unleashed: Time Management Strategies for Entrepreneurs
82. The Problem Solver's Toolkit: Creative Solutions for Business Challenges
83. The Future is Now: Emerging Trends in Business
84. The Curious Explorer: A Child's Guide to Scientific Discovery
85. Digital Pioneers: Empowering Kids in the Tech World
86. The Young Philosopher's Guide: Exploring Life's Big Questions
87. Finding Your Voice: Communication Skills for Confident Kids
88. Nature's Playground: A Child's Guide to Outdoor Adventure
89. Growing a Greener Tomorrow: A Guide to Tree Planting & Conservation
90. Driving with Purpose: Ethical Choices on the Road
91. The Healing Touch: Cultivating Compassion in Healthcare
92. Navigating the Digital Landscape: Ethics in the Age of Social Media
93. The Ethical Closet: A Guide to Sustainable Fashion
94. The Mindful Voyager: Sustainable Travel Practices
95. The Feminine Divine: Honoring the Goddesses of India
96. Sacred Sounds: Chanting Your Way to Inner Peace
97. The Yoga Path: Uniting with the Divine Within
98. Rites of Passage: Creating Meaningful Ceremonies
99. The Chakra System: A Map of Inner Transformation
100. Spiritual Sangha: Finding Community through Satsang and

Bhajan
101. Pilgrimage of the Soul: Spiritual Journeys in India

ততত

Contact

Dr. Minakshi Bansal
Social Activist
Ahmedabad, Gujarat, Bharat
minakshiindiag20@yahoo.com

ᐳᐳᐳ

|| LOKAHA SAMASTHAHA SUKHINO BHAVANTU ||